MW00698575

Deliberately Me:

A journey for those seeking contentment

in a deliberate God

Lee Johnson

Deliberately Me: A journey for those seeking contentment in a deliberate God. Copyright © 2018 by Lee Johnson.

Scripture references noted "AMP" are taken from the Holy Bible, Amplified Version. Copyright © 1954, 1958, 1962, 1964, 1965, 1987 by The Lockman Foundation. All rights reserved.

Scripture references noted "KJV" are taken from the Holy Bible, King James Version. Public Domain.

Scripture references noted "MSG" are taken from The Message. Copyright © 1993, 1994, 1995, 1996, 2000, 2001, 2002. Used by permission of NavPress Publishing Group. All rights reserved.

Scripture references noted "NASB" are taken from the New American Standard Bible® Copyright©1960, 1962, 1963, 1968, 1971, 1972, 1973, 1975, 1977, 1995 by The Lockman Foundation. Used by permission. All rights reserved.

Scripture references noted "NIV" are taken from the Holy Bible, New International Version. Copyright © 1973, 1978, 1984 by International Bible Society. Used by permission of Zondervan Bible Publishers. All rights reserved.

Scripture references noted "NKJV" are taken from the Holy Bible, New King James Version. Copyright © 1982 by Thomas Nelson, Inc. Used by permission. All rights reserved.

Scripture references noted "NLT" are taken from the Holy Bible, New Living Translation. Copyright © 1996. Used by permission of Tyndale House Publishers, Inc., Wheaton, Illinois 60189. All rights reserved.

All rights reserved. No portion of this book may be reproduced, stored in a retrieval system, or transmitted in any form or by any means—electronic, mechanical, photocopy, recording, scanning, or other—except for brief quotations in critical reviews or articles, without the prior written permission of the publisher.

Publishing consultant: Obieray Rogers (www.rubiopublishing.com)

ISBN 978-1731163554

Response to *Deliberately Me*

"In *Deliberately Me,* women are challenged to face our insecurities, something most of us avoid. We are then provided with strategies to overcome them and walk out our purpose."—C.B.

"This is a thought-provoking book, forcing you to look at your true inner self and your relationship with God. It's perfect for the girl or woman who needs to find out who she is."—K.C.

"Lee Johnson is an inspiring spiritually-led woman of God who brings to life her passion for teaching others the Word of God in her new book *Deliberately Me.* Her book takes readers on a journey of deep reflection of their past and present and helps them discover the future God has in store for them once they focus on the mindset of being "deliberately" themselves."—H.J.

"I had a chance to read *Deliberately Me* when I was in a very deep pit. The author's godly words of wisdom spoke to my heart, causing me to realize how much God loves and wants the best for me."—A.H.

"Lee invites you for real girl talk. You will come away loved on by God and wiser for the journey." —N.H.

Dedication

To the two most important young ladies in my life:
Dejahne and Tahlia.

I dedicate *Deliberate Me* to you because without you I wouldn't have learned so many things about myself (good and well. . .you know). You both have taught me the Lord's grace through your patience for me as your mother.

Your devotion to each other, love for your family, and continued dedication to drive me bonkers, truly blesses my life.
You have always been my silent push to do better
for myself and for the world.

Thank you . . .

To my Mom (Abigail), for being my biggest supporter and encouraging me to write since I was in elementary school.

To Harolyn, for being my accountability partner, and your persistence in ensuring I didn't become distracted from the Lord's vision.

To Chandrika, for re-connecting me with Obieray to have my book published.

To the *Deliberately Me* critique group—Adhanet, April, Audrey, Chandrika, Harolyn, Kelli, and Nan—for your commitment to read and provide feedback for improvements.

To the best team on earth—Team Victorious (you know who you are)—for your continued prayers for me and each other.

Q.U.E.E.N.S

(Quiet, Unique, Elegant, Everlasting, Noble, Sisters)

From my perspective, Christian women are not fulfilling their purpose as followers of Christ. We live in a society where many women experience overwhelming situations that lead to lack of confidence, low self-esteem, depression, drug abuse, single motherhood, and, overall, lack of purpose as a woman.

My passion is to not only minister to the unsaved, but to help the women of God reach their full potential. We are not called to be another woman sitting cute in a chair (at church or work), but we should be better mothers, sisters, daughters, aunts, wives, neighbors, strangers, mentors, co-workers, employees, and leaders in our community. We should be able to read, learn, and apply the Word of God to our lives daily. We should be doing more than just listening to someone else preach the Word of God. Overtime, we should desire to use our gifts to minister and assist with someone else's development at work, home, school, and so forth.

The Lord's vision for me is to do more than lead women to Christ; the goal is to help women live a virtuous life for Him, and to be a witness for the lost and other Christian women. So, how do we do this?

We do this through Women's Ministry. Please understand, Women's Ministry doesn't happen only in a building where we discuss God's Word and share tears together. Women's Ministry is not even something that needs a title or group. Women's Ministry starts when a woman of God chooses to follow Jesus and bring a few sisters along to meet Him as well. Women's Ministry is the desire to learn and live by God's Word, and then become a true disciple by growing, loving, and sharing your growth to help others grow. It is an experience that allows all women to grow in Christ, to live better lives, to think better about themselves, and to love other women, instead of being jealous or envious because they do not recognize the power within.

Women's Ministry is an experience that all women need, but it is not happening enough. Women's Ministry should be a mentorship, a sisterhood, and an unlimited, powerful tool where you accept your gifts and share them with the world. Choose to join the Women's Ministry for Christ and start discipling other women!

Women's Ministry should be a ministry that propels ordinary women into extraordinary QUEENS—**Q**uiet, **U**nique, **E**legant, **E**verlasting, **N**oble, **S**isters.

CONTENTS

Introduction

Would you agree that our world offers so much to see and experience? There are things to explore like new restaurants, shopping malls, the local art exhibit, an exciting car show, or even monthly festivals. There are the up-and-coming business owners who seek the passions and skills of new employees to help broaden their company's future.

However, for some, our world can look very different depending on the perspective of the person. You don't have to read this book to know we live in a world that tells women that being attractive includes being an acceptable height and weight; your hair must be a certain way, and your makeup must be the latest trend or brand. Some of us may even feel pressured on our jobs to keep up with someone else's wardrobe (which could mean expensive decisions and brands we normally don't buy). The world even dictates the colors we choose throughout the year with the changing seasons. (I was once told to not wear turtleneck sweaters in April, although it was 20 degrees outside! What else would I wear?) The world also tries to dictate the type of characteristics we should have in order to become successful. But, how can the world define success, when my success will look different than the success of the almost eight billion people occupying the planet?

For some of you, the last paragraph holds true because you allow everyone (family, friends, co-workers, and so on) to dictate your life. You allow the magazine aisle to make you think twice about the donuts in your cart. Or, maybe your parents have caused you to second-guess how you stand, talk, and pursue dating.

Don't freak out about it because there is good news! You can stop looking for yourself in a book and other women. You can accept that the qualities you have been given inside and out were not a mistake. You can learn that your past preconceptions are all in your head and do not align to God's thoughts about you.

How so? Well, take a deep breath and pause for a moment. We live in a world where many women allow a *who* to dictate the colors they wear, the makeup they buy, the school their children attend, the sports they play, the restaurants where they dine, and the list goes on and on. You may be wondering who I am referencing when I say *who*: it is whomever you're allowing to dictate your life.

This book is for women trying to overcome insecurities and barriers holding them back from their true design. The insecurity may be the woman living next door who appears to have everything you don't. Perhaps she is married with the perfect husband and well-behaved children. She has a great job, makes a lot of money, and receives all the rewards. She is the fitness expert with a body shaped by Zeus, which leaves you wondering how you were skipped over. She has great health, never gets sick, and is always optimistic. You know, she's the woman who pretty much gets on your nerves, even though she has done absolutely nothing, except exist in the same world as you!

This book is for the woman who needs to be set free to live and to enjoy her life without comparison to anyone else. To be free from the shame of wanting to be someone else. To be free from the constant thoughts of what else can I do to be better. To be free from believing that others are better than you. Just free!

News flash! God has already created you in a specific way. There is nothing (no thing) you can add to an already perfected diamond. You were handcrafted by Almighty God. Everything you are is everything you need to be. You only need to be you. You just need to say, "I am going to be *Deliberately Me!*"

Chapter 1

Deliberate:

Learning to do things on purpose

Words are only powerful if you understand their meaning and usage. Throughout this book, I want you to focus on the definitions and Scriptures mentioned in each chapter. Let's begin by journeying together through some definitions for being deliberate. Yes, I understand many of you already know the definition for the word, but it is important to understand in detail how you can be deliberate in every aspect of your life.

I discovered an example of being deliberate as a young girl. I learned young boys premeditate, plan, and intentionally hit girls they like without rhyme or reason. They will chase and harass young girls they find interesting. Even though I am older and can comprehend those intentions from long ago, I still do not understand their method for getting a girl to like them. But this is an approach that is deliberate.

Dictionary.com describes the word *deliberate* as "carefully weighed or considered; studied; intentional." Let's discuss the words "careful," "considered," and "intentional."

These words suggest that being deliberate requires effort for something to happen.

Dictionary.com also defines *deliberate* as "carefully thought out in advance." This description emphasizes the importance of thinking about something before you do it. When you plan an event, do you think of every possible scenario or settle immediately on the first idea that comes to mind?

Finally, Merriam-Webster.com defines *deliberate* as to "think about or discuss something very carefully in order to make a decision."

Which definition best describes your understanding of the word? In order to be deliberate, you must carefully consider every thought (idea) before a decision is made, especially if this action affects you or others in a negative way.

In the Greek language, the word for deliberate is *skópimos*—spelled σκόπιμος. This source defines *deliberate* as "intentional, desirable, expedient, willful, and purposeful." The Greek definition is similar to the previous examples, but did you catch the new word, *desirable*? I don't know about you, but many things I do deliberately are not things I've desired to complete such as work or laundry, dishes, washing my daughter's hair, or choosing salad over French fries. I've never prayed to God and said, "I desire to wash clothes, and spend an hour washing and blow drying my daughter's hair." Interesting enough, the word *desirable* is used to describe deliberate. You'll learn more about God's desire for you in a later chapter.

Finally, the last way to view the word *deliberate* is by using synonyms. I love the Microsoft® Word tool that allows you to view various synonyms by right-clicking and selecting synonyms. The last sentence was for those women who are not friends with technology.

I obtained the following list from the Internet, which was easier than cracking open my thesaurus. Of course, there are many more options, but I deliberately chose the list below:

Advised	**Done On Purpose**	Predetermined	Schemed
Aforethought	Express	Premeditated	Scrupulous
Calculated	**Fixed**	Prepense	Studied
Careful	Intended	Projected	Studious
Cautious	Judged	Provident	Thought Out
Cold-Blooded	**Meticulous**	Prudent	Thoughtful
Conscious	**Planned**	Purposed	**Voluntary**
Considered	Pondered	**Purposeful**	Wary
Cut-And-Dried	Prearranged	Purposive	Weighed
Designed	Predesigned	Reasoned	**Willful**
Designful	**Predeterminate**	Resolved	With Forethought

If you pay close attention, you will notice synonym-like words from the definitions. I highlighted a few that I thought were good examples.

Exercise 1.1: Write some examples you think are good synonyms for being deliberate.

_____

_____

_____

_____

_____

_____

_____

Exercise 1.2: What are some specific things you deliberately (consider) do when starting the work week? Do you review the weekly tasks to **prioritize** which items to complete first? Do you **review** your child's appointments to ensure you arrive on time? Do you **think** (intentional) about the drive into work and map out the routes to avoid traffic? Do you **carefully** plan the weekly menu for dinner (what days to cook or eat out)? Jot a few examples of specific things you deliberately do throughout the week.

_____

_____

_____

_____

_____

_____

_____

Displaying a deliberate nature doesn't equal perfection, but it does mean being careful in selecting a method for accomplishing something. Perhaps it means attempting to be successful at deliverables that are important to you.

I don't know about you, but I am deliberate in planning out the things I care about (or at least I try to be). Children's parties are a good example. Many parents take the planning of a baby's first birthday seriously. Why? Because *"Children are a gift from the Lord; they are a reward from him"* (Psalm 127:3, NLT). Parents not only value their children, but also enjoy sharing this celebration with family and friends. So, whether you throw a party at your house or someplace else, first birthdays are significant, as well as every year after. Birthdays are so important that many put great emphasis on the milestone years like Sweet Sixteen, 18, 21, 30, 50, and beyond. I have a cousin who celebrates her birthday the entire month. In doing this, she is being deliberate in celebrating not only her birthday but life itself.

Exercise 1.3: Can you think of anyone from the Bible who demonstrated a deliberate attitude? (I'm sure Jesus comes to mind, but you are not allowed to use Him because this would be too easy.) List a few Bible characters who were deliberate.

_____
_____
_____
_____
_____
_____
_____

Exercise 1.4: List how being deliberate (intentional) worked out for them. What were the negative and/or positive results?

_____
_____
_____
_____
_____
_____
_____

When I completed this action item, I struggled with listing someone, not because of a lack of options in the Bible, but because there are so many. I ended up choosing the apostle Paul (formerly known as Saul).

If you have ever read any of Paul's letters, you can experience his intentional desire to win people to Christ. For those already following Christ, He provided godly practices to live by according to God's will.

Some of the letters were written to rebuke (not condemn) ungodly behavior, and to remind followers the hope we have in Christ. Paul intentionally reminds us to stay away from a legalistic and hypocritical lifestyle. He states how to treat your enemies and to be thankful in all things. He intentionally reminded the people he visited, how much he loved them and cared about their relationship with God. He even reminds us to renew our minds daily to avoid conforming to this world (Romans 12:2). Paul talks about the importance of gifts and their benefit to the Kingdom.

Paul was always deliberate in his actions toward his brothers and sisters. Don't believe me? Read the passage below and pay close attention to the statements I've emphasized in bold lettering.

PHILIPPIANS 1:7-11 (MSG):

*It's not at all fanciful for me to think this way about you. **My prayers and hopes have deep roots** in reality. You have, after all, stuck with me all the way from the time I was thrown in jail, put on trial, and came out of it in one piece. All along you have experienced with me the most generous help from God. He knows how much I love and miss you these days. **Sometimes I think I feel as strongly about you as Christ does!** So, this is my prayer: **that your love will flourish and that you will not only love much but well. Learn to love appropriately.** You need to use your head and test your feelings so that your love is sincere and intelligent, not sentimental gush. Live a lover's life, circumspect and exemplary, a life Jesus will be proud of: bountiful in fruits from the soul, **making Jesus Christ attractive to all,** getting everyone involved in the glory and praise of God.* (Emphasis mine)

God (through the Holy Spirit) deliberately chose you and then gave you gifts to benefit His will. Gifting is a deliberate act from God. If you are still in unbelief, read Romans 12:3-8 and all of 1 Corinthians 12. Better yet, read all the books of the Bible. You will find many intentional acts from God and his people throughout Scripture. One thing to remember is those who chose to be intentional about their relationship with God always yielded positive results. This doesn't mean the journey was always roses and

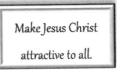

Make Jesus Christ attractive to all.

sunshine, or unicorns and rainbows, or even cheese and sprinkles, but those whose intentions were aligned with the Lord always yielded fruit.

Exercise 1.5: List one story where God or Jesus showed a deliberate behavior. There is one caveat, you can't use John 3:16, NIV: *"God so loved the world that he gave his one and only son,"* or 1 John 4:10, NLT: *"This is real love—not that we loved God, but that he loved us and sent his Son as a sacrifice to take away our sins,"* or any other Scriptures mentioning the act of Jesus' death and resurrection. That would be too easy! Most of us understand that God was being intentional, deliberate, and a loving Father for saving us. Choose another event to illustrate an act of being deliberate. Also, list why you think their actions were deliberate.

_____

_____

_____

_____

_____

_____

_____

There are a variety of ways of exploring the word *deliberate*, and we have only just begun. Our discussion of the importance of being deliberate in everything we do continues.

Chapter 2

Deliberately Her:

Learning to be you despite her

We now move on to discuss something other than definitions and synonyms. I hope the last chapter provided a visual for the word *deliberate* because now we get to talk about *her* and you. Who is *she* and why are we focusing on someone other than you? *She* is the person mentioned in the Introduction; the one you think was intentionally sent by God to annoy you because *she* appears to be everything you are not.

Before we focus on *her*, let's talk about you to identify your feelings toward yourself. How do you feel most mornings when you wake up? I am not talking about whether you got enough rest; this is important but not the focal point. I mean do you wake up ready to tackle the day as you? You know. . .you!

Let's borrow a name; let's use Mindy. Every morning Mindy wakes up ready to go to work as a fifth-grade teacher at a local elementary school. She teaches both Math and Reading. Mindy graduated three years ago and has only been teaching for two years; she always looks forward to learning from fellow colleagues. She also enjoys learning different methods to assist her students with their education. Although she loves her job, Mindy has experienced hostility due to being fresh out of college and new to the school district. However, she doesn't let this behavior bother her and has a great outlook for her career.

Now, back to you. When you read this summary, is this you? Are you Mindy? Let me help you pick out things to ponder from this story. Mindy graduated from college. Mindy is doing something she passionately enjoys. Mindy loves learning and helping others. Mindy is experiencing issues with other teachers, but she doesn't let the negative behavior of others affect her teaching. Truthfully, not many of us are Mindy, but can you answer yes to any of the questions below?

1. Are you naturally happy and excited, looking forward to tackling the day?
2. Do you enjoy where you work or your current job?
3. Do you enjoy learning?
4. Are you experiencing difficult times?
5. Regardless of problems, do you tackle them your way or worry too much about how someone else would have resolved the situation?
6. **Do you enjoy being you?**

Now, pause for a moment. No, seriously, pause and think about the last question. Maybe grab a cup of tea, coffee, or water because if you're going to continue reading this book, I need you to be honest with yourself.

On a scale of one to ten, how much do you love yourself? Do you like your complexion, hair, eyes, voice, family, upbringing, friendships (social life), and personal energy? Do you like your relationships with people at church, work, home, school, and so forth? Do you have healthy relationships with people? Are you comfortable around the people you see daily, or do you find yourself comparing your life to theirs? This comparison is not always an outward act but sometimes an internal discussion with yourself at home or as you drive to work. More so, by the time you get to work, you are upset by your preconceived thoughts about *her* or them.

I ask these questions because some women instantly get defensive and respond with, "I love everything about myself." But, if this is true, then why are you so irritated by *her*? Why are you trying to have everything *she* has, wear everything *she* does, go everywhere *she* goes, befriend everyone *she* is friends with?

Or, perhaps you are the opposite. You despise everything *she* does and make negative comments about *her* style and friends. You dislike *her* but are never able to provide a rational reason for your dislike except your common statement, "I just don't like *her*!"

I hate to break this to you, and I'll attempt to let you down gently. *She* does not desire to be you because *she* is too busy being deliberately *her*! For the most part, women are not strategizing at night how to beat you, how to take your job, how to have a better husband, and how to have better disciplined children than you. They don't care how many friends you have on Facebook, Twitter, or Instagram, or whether you're a great cook. They don't even care about the new car you drive or the fake designer purse you claim to have purchased in New York.

> They are focused on what pleases them.

Do you know why they don't care? They are not intimidated by you because they are too distracted by being happy. You are not even an afterthought. They are focused on what pleases them and those in their world, not yours.

The truth is, *she* is not impressed that you're a great cook because *her* husband knew he married a hot dog and Ramen noodle kind of gal. The *she* in your life has always been okay cooking once a week, and it works because *her* husband cooks the other six days of the week. You thought all this time *she* was being fake, but *she* is really a genuinely happy person. Have you ever thought the *she* in your life is more concerned about *her*self than impressing you? Better yet, did you forget *she* lives in this world and must work hard just like you?

There are very few—if any—women contemplating competition with you; but this is why there are therapists in the world: to assist women who feel the need to compare and compete with everyone they meet. But should this be your problem? No!

Let's be honest. Is it possible that you have exaggerated *her* actions just a little? I would even venture to say that you have somehow conjured in your mind that every woman in the world is out to get you, as if from birth your name was planted in *her* mind, and this became *her* life's mission to seek you out. *She* deliberately went to the same high school as you. *She* deliberately went to the same college and applied to the same company. *She* deliberately found a decent husband and had children just to make you mad. *She* deliberately exercises just to be in better shape than you. *She* even joined the same gym as you, goes to the same grocery store, and had the nerve to enroll *her* kids in the same elementary school. Oh! What nerve! *She* even accepted Jesus Christ. *She* wanted to follow in your footsteps since you became a follower of Christ. Really?

Exercise 2.1: It's time for a chapter break because I sense some hostility coming from you. I was going to suggest re-reading the last paragraph; but if this has upset you, then take a break. Remember, we need to be honest with ourselves. If this has hit a nerve, then please list what's upsetting you about these statements before continuing to read. If you're unable to relate, then list items some of your friends (or family members) are exaggerating about other women. Maybe you can help them identify their preconceived and exaggerated thoughts.

_____

_____

_____

_____

_____

_____

_____

Have you ever thought the *she* in your life has learned to be exactly what God has called *her* to be? Confident, fun, loving, out of balance at times but patient. Trendy yet different. Lovable but direct, when necessary. Noticeable because she doesn't seek attention, and others are drawn to *her* because *she* is genuine and unique.

Ask yourself, what really bothers you about *her*? Is *she* everything you wish you could be? I hope not because God didn't create you to be Mindy. Mindy is supposed to be Mindy, and you are supposed to be you. You were deliberately created to be you, not *her*. There goes that word again, deliberate. If you would stop using energy to dislike *her*, then you could channel that energy toward being more of you. Plus, the possibility of channeling your energy into loving yourself and not worrying about others would be far less painful.

MATTHEW 6:25-34 (NIV):

> *"Therefore, I tell you, do not worry about your life, what you will eat or drink; or about your body, what you will wear. Is not life more than food, and the body more than clothes? Look at the birds of the air; they do not sow or reap or store away in barns, and yet your heavenly Father feeds them. Are you not much more valuable than they? Can any one of you by worrying add a single hour to your life? And why do you worry about clothes? See how the flowers of the field grow. They do not labor or spin. Yet I tell you that not even Solomon in all his splendor was dressed like one of these. If that is how God clothes the grass of the field, which is here today and tomorrow is thrown into the fire, will he not much more clothe you—you of little faith? So, do not worry, saying, 'What shall we eat?' or 'What shall we drink?' or 'What shall we wear?' For the pagans run after all these things, and your heavenly Father knows that you need them. But seek first his kingdom and his righteousness, and all these things will be given to you as well. Therefore, do not worry about tomorrow, for tomorrow will worry about itself. Each day has enough trouble of its own."*
> (Emphasis mine)

When you walk in the park, have you ever seen two birds compete for having the best nest? Have you ever seen Blue Jays rebuild their nest because they observed the Cardinals using branches from an oak tree? Have you ever seen a cat compete with her sibling for who is the cleanest by counting who licks her fur the most throughout the day? Did you ever witness an older dog tease a younger dog, because the master petted him first? (Hmm! On second thought, we should scratch the dog example because they can be jealous at times.) Come on, ladies, this is supposed to make you laugh, although animals really do not carry the same cares as humans.

Matthew 6:25-34 doesn't mean God is going to grocery shop for you or cook your family's meals. It doesn't mean you can go to work in your birthday suit or use a lack of judgment by wearing jeans and a t-shirt to a job interview (unless specified by the interviewer). The passage is not suggesting that if you stop worrying, everything you need will fall from the sky; however, the Word is reminding us that competition or alliance with ungodly things will lead to destruction. Let's make it simple: Worrying is the opposite of trusting God! When you are worried about *her* and how *she* looks, dresses, acts, and is perceived by others, then you have put your trust in worldly things, instead of believing you are just as valuable.

Worrying or trying to compete for someone else's things is sinful. In the Bible, it's called coveting. *"You shall not covet your neighbor's house. You shall not covet your neighbor's wife, or his male or female servant, his ox or donkey, or anything that belongs to your neighbor"* (Exodus 20:17, NIV). Did you understand the last

> Worrying is the opposite of trusting God!

sentence? Everything about *her* belongs to *her,* and we do not have the right to be angry about the blessings bestowed upon *her.* Why? Because God made you to be something amazing as well. The sad news is that you are so consumed with desire for something that does not belong to you, which blinds you from realizing your own blessings.

There is nothing wrong when the people around you have things you desire. God never intended for you to feel ashamed and offended, or to have an unhealthy competitive nature for things others have. God designed you to be confident through Christ, so you can accept everyone, including *Deliberately Her*. *She* is only being what God handcrafted *her* to be, and you should do the same.

Exercise 2.2: Re-read Matthew 6:25-34. How does this passage make you feel? How do you compare yourself to other women? What are you coveting that is causing a sinful attitude toward *her*, yourself, and others?

_____

_____

_____

_____

_____

_____

_____

Chapter 3

Deliberately Confident:

Learning to be humbly confident through Christ

In chapter two, we discussed *her,* and hopefully you understand *she* was never the problem. Your perception, upbringing, and too much (or not enough) understanding have led you to believe the grass is always greener on the other side. Well, it's not! If the grass is greener, then you should know by now there is no need to cross over to the other side. All you need to do is pray for God to water your own grass to become greener without trying to become someone else.

PSALM 37:3-6 (NIV):

> *Trust in the Lord and do good; dwell in the land and enjoy safe pasture. Take delight in the Lord, and he will give you the desires of your heart. Commit your way to the Lord; trust in him and he will do this.*

PSALM 37:3-6 (MSG):

> *Get insurance with God and do a good deed, settle down and stick to your last. Keep company with God, get in on the best. Open up before God, keep nothing back; he'll do whatever needs to be done:* **He'll validate your life in the clear light of day and stamp you with approval at high noon.** (Emphasis mine)

Once again, this doesn't mean God will give you everything you ask for; but it does mean if you trust in Him and if you submit those desires to God, He will always provide what's necessary, permanent, and everlasting to benefit you and not distract you from your purpose.

I mentioned the word *confident* in the last chapter, which means I feel a defining moment coming on. Yep, let's do it. Merriam-Webster.com defines the word *confidence* as a "feeling or belief that you can do something well or succeed at something. The feeling of being certain that something will happen or that something is true."

The Greek word for confidence is εμπιστοσύνη— pronounced *empistosýni*. This means "confidence, trust, reliance, trustiness." Dictionary.com defines it as "full trust; belief in the powers, trustworthiness, or reliability of a person or thing." The statements "full trust" and reliability of a person reminds me of Hebrews 11:1-3 (NLT):

> *Faith shows the reality of what we hope for; it is the evidence of things we cannot see. Through their faith, the people in days of old earned a good reputation. By faith we understand that the entire universe was formed at God's command, that what we now see did not come from anything that can be seen.*

The Scripture from Hebrews confirms we can be confident that our God did everything the Bible states because He is trustworthy and reliable. Do the descriptions for confidence fit your personality? Do you think happy thoughts for success or always the worse of your capabilities? For example, when it comes to interviewing or casual conversations about work or personal life, are you able to easily articulate your strengths? You know, those things you are good at. **Are you able to sell *you?***

I am not trying to overwhelm you, and this is not an interview. I just want to know if it's easy to talk about yourself freely without hesitation.

Let's try a different approach. Answer the following questions. When you walk, do you stand up straight with your head lifted, or do you look at the ground? Do you make eye contact with others? Do you smile or avoid eye contact and look away? Lord knows I am no psychologist, but I always find it interesting to watch how people walk. Smiling versus not smiling. Slumped versus good posture. Timid versus strong. Confrontational versus inviting. Confidence versus arrogance. These behaviors have led me to wonder why people act a certain way. Did you know there is a difference between self-esteem and self-confidence?

Exercise 3.1: Define below your thoughts on the difference between self-esteem and self-confidence.

_____
_____
_____
_____
_____

SELF-ESTEEM VERSUS SELF-CONFIDENCE

According to an article I discovered at www.healthyplace.com, "Self-esteem refers to how you feel about yourself overall; how much esteem, positive regard or self-love you have. Self-confidence is how you feel about your abilities and can vary from situation to situation."

So, let's go back to the topic of walking with your head down. I am not suggesting that people who walk with their head down are necessarily lacking something, but I do believe our mood can affect how we flow throughout our day. For example, you may have high self-esteem, but your confidence level may be low due to a recent job performance review. You may be confident in your job because you are the go-to person, yet, you are the doormat at home because your husband and children don't respect you. There is a connection between the two, and one should feed the other.

Self-esteem ➤ Self-confidence or Self-confidence ➤ Self-esteem

Personally, I feel better when I hold my head high, even on a bad day. Holding my head upright encourages me to smile and acknowledge people as they walk by. When I walk with my head down, I don't feel confident and prefer to not engage others. Also, when my head is down, my posture is off and so is my personal energy. When I allow my emotions to affect my flow, it not only upsets my mood, but it alters my interaction with others. It can also modify my thoughts in how I deal with situations. When you hold your head down, are you more positive and confident, believing the best outcome? Do you walk in expectation of the Lord's provisions? Still not getting the message? Well, there is a song based on Scripture that should not only lead to worship but empowerment when you really listen to the words. Do you know the Scripture-turned song I am referencing?

PSALM 121:1-8 (KJV):

> *I **will lift up mine eyes** unto the hills, **from whence cometh my help. My help cometh from the Lord**, which made heaven and earth. He will not suffer thy foot to be moved: he that keepeth thee will not slumber. Behold, he that keepeth Israel shall neither slumber nor sleep. The **Lord is thy keeper**: the Lord is thy shade upon thy right hand. The sun shall not smite thee by day, nor the moon by night. The **Lord shall preserve thee** from all evil: he shall preserve thy soul. The Lord shall preserve thy going out and thy coming in from this time forth, and even for evermore.* (Emphasis mine)

When you read Psalm 121 or listen to the song *My Help (Cometh from the Lord)* by Jackie Gouche Farris (2008), are you reminded to lift your head high in the belief that God is your help? If you truly believe the message of Psalm 121, then you should learn to walk confidently by faith that God is your help. This means God can help you with any challenges you face. God shall keep you from evil and preserve your soul (v. 7). He preserves your coming and going (v. 8). The Free Dictionary.com describes the word *preserve* as to "keep from injury, harm; to protect. To keep in perfect or unaltered condition." It's so amazing our heavenly Father is devoted to preserving us daily. Hopefully, this will raise your spirits to lift your head, because you can be confident in His abilities and not worry about yours.

I got a little sidetracked regarding our posture, but just know our physical demeanor can affect our mood. Since we already discussed this, let me repeat a question from earlier: Can you speak freely about yourself without hesitation? Are you proud of what you've become? What do you see yourself becoming? **Are you happy with what you see?**

Let me share something personal. Since I was a little girl, I had always desired to raise children with a husband. The fact is, I became a parent with children out of wedlock. Some folks use the phrase "single parent" as if we're outcasts and need pity. Let me correct that myth. Single does not mean weak, inadequate, or powerless. Single parent means you are not married—or were married and are now divorced—and the children do not have both parents living in the same home. Single means One, Uno, Un.

What is my point? For a long time, it was difficult for me to speak freely about parenting, because I felt ashamed due to my relationship status—not married. With time, the Lord has shown me I am valuable, and a good parent regardless of my single status. He taught me to stop focusing on the *Deliberately Her* in my life and learn to just be *Deliberately Lee*.

Exercise 3.2: Answer the following questions while thinking about how confident you are in yourself:

1. Are you able to speak up for yourself without hesitation (in a respectful manner)? I chose the word respectful because confidence does not degrade others nor think lowly of them.
2. Are you happy or ashamed when you discuss family, your career, children, hobbies, and so forth?
3. Are there certain questions you dread to answer about your life?

4. How would you describe yourself?

Please don't continue until you have honestly answered these questions and spoken to God about them. Write your thoughts, and then talk to God and write the results.

_____

_____

_____

_____

_____

_____

_____

Do you remember Moses? Before you point out he was a leader of the Israelites and God used him to free his people, you need to remember in the beginning, Moses was not a confident man. God had to constantly encourage him toward his full capabilities.

EXODUS 4:8-17 (NKJV):

> *"Then it will be, if they do not believe you, nor heed the message of the first sign, that they may believe the message of the latter sign. And it shall be, if they do not believe even these two signs, or listen to your voice, that you shall take water from the river and pour it on the dry land. The water which you take from the river will become blood on the dry land."*
>
> *Then Moses said to the LORD, "O my Lord, I am not eloquent, neither before nor since You have spoken to Your servant; but I am slow of speech and slow of tongue."*
>
> *So the LORD said to him, "Who has made man's mouth? Or who makes the mute, the deaf, the seeing, or the blind? Have not I, the LORD? Now*

therefore, go, and I will be with your mouth and teach you what you shall say."

But he said, "O my Lord, please send by the hand of whomever else You may send." So the anger of the LORD was kindled against Moses, and He said: "Is not Aaron the Levite your brother? I know that he can speak well. And look, he is also coming out to meet you. When he sees you, he will be glad in his heart. Now you shall speak to him and put the words in his mouth. And I will be with your mouth and with his mouth, and I will teach you what you shall do. So he shall be your spokesman to the people. And he himself shall be as a mouth for you, and you shall be to him as God. And you shall take this rod in your hand, with which you shall do the signs."

Even with God's affirmation, Moses was still not confident (trusting) that God could do miraculous things through him. It's interesting because even though a bush burned (not just any bush but a burning bush with the Lord's voice!), a staff turned into a snake, seas were parted, and food fell from heaven, Moses still struggled with confidence.

I'm not talking about the kind of confidence that you or I can attain by ourselves. I am speaking of the confidence in knowing God created you and doesn't require you to be something more than what you are. Yes, skills, experience, education, and many other things are important—and God uses them all—but true confidence is the ability to be you without apology.

> Confidence does not degrade others nor think lowly of them.

Remember, godly confidence does not mean being unapologetic when we display the ungodly behaviors of rudeness and demoralization.

I emphasize confidence *through* Christ because at some point over the years Christians began to follow worldly standards of confidence. This confidence throws people under the bus at any cost to move up a level at work. This confidence says because I am a woman in a specific field, I am required to be aggressive (instead of assertive), demeaning, or insensitive in order to be noticed or appreciated. Worldly confidence is blinded by pride and doesn't require an apologetic nature. This kind of confidence believes because I am a vice president, I can ignore anyone below my executive level. This kind of confidence is insensitive to the restaurant server, even though she or he didn't cause the mistake with your food. This confidence believes that because I have a nice car, a good salary, and a lot of stuff, I am better than the homeless man or woman on the street. This attitude says, "I made it, why can't you?"

I'm sure you know exactly who I am talking about. Is this you? You may have fought hard to obtain what you have, but how many relationships did you destroy to get there? How many spirits did you crush with your words? How many nights do you cry because you are friendless, and no one enjoys your presence? People gossip behind your back not because you're a great leader but because of all the bridges you've burned. Anyone claiming to be a follower of Christ should follow His example of confidence and not the worldly ways that are highly praised. You should run from worldly confidence because it's solely based on the view of man, which can lead to destruction.

On the other hand, being *Deliberately Confident* (through Christ) is our expectation. Deliberate confidence is knowing the right response is a soft word versus a direct blow that leads to anger. Deliberate confidence is being a single parent and knowing your children deserve the best like any other child.

It is confidence in not having a college degree, yet still able to educate others. It is confidence that doesn't require a title at work because you're capable of being an influential leader without one. The confidence to be friends with people who are outcasts, a different shade, and a larger size than you. The confidence in yourself to feel just as good in jogging pants as you would in a designer dress. Regardless of your family background, shortcomings, mistakes, failures, and ungodly disasters, you still can be *Deliberately Confident,* just like Jesus, because you choose to deliberately trust Him every day.

ASPECTS OF BEING DELIBERATELY CONFIDENT

The first chapter of the book of Genesis states that everything God created was good. Yes, you were a sinner but because of Christ, you have everything you need to be confident in everything you do. You are good. Do you believe that? Well, let me help you with a definition. Merriam-Webster.com defines *good* as "of a favorable character or tendency, good news. Of high quality." Wow! High quality! God is saying you are valuable and of high quality.

If you walk with your head down, stop it! Nothing good can come from looking at the ground and avoiding eye contact, emotions, and smiles from other people. If God wanted us to walk with our heads down, He would have created our bodies with an arch to look downward. Some animals walk on four legs and even they hold their head high. My cat Izzie is a spoiled brat, but even she walks around the house proudly, knowing she is loved. Izzie walks proudly because she has confidence in herself and me because I faithfully feed her everyday (with treats).

I mentioned *with treats* as a reminder that the Lord not only provides what we **need** but He'll sometimes even give us what we **want**. My Izzie could live a long, healthy life not even knowing what a treat is; yet, I give them to her because I love her and want her to know she is a good kitty (of high quality).

You should be confident that the Lord will continually provide for you.

Be proud of who you are. Are you a stay-at-home Mom, Farmer, Home Health Aide, Administrative Assistant, Coach, Mentor, Policewoman, Teacher, Public Service Employee, Government Official, Retail Representative, Banker, or Manager? Do you have a career or are you still figuring out what you want to be when you grow up? Who cares what path you have chosen, or how you ended up in this moment called today. Be happy. People are happy to see you and spend time with you. Be happy and believe you have many things to offer this world. You can be happy because the Lord has said you are of high quality! Be you! Be *Deliberately Confident!* Or, can I shout out to the young folks? Do you, Boo!

I mentioned earlier in the chapter that there is a connection between self-esteem and self-confidence. I also revealed that one should feed the other. I believe self-esteem should always feed confidence. Confidence shifts depending on the situation, but someone who is constantly building their self-esteem can never be shaken.

I have known women with great jobs, beautiful homes, an awesome salary, and a patient husband; yet, they intentionally offend the men and women in their lives. They're always telling everyone what they should and shouldn't do, how they should dress, and what they need to do to get ahead in life. They appear to care but are exhibiting nit-picky, opinionated behavior.

Everyone has an opinion, but a self-content woman doesn't spend her time trying to fix everyone else. Most of us know at least one woman like this; they may even be related. You know the type. This is the confident woman at work who gets promoted, yet allows every man in her life to take, take, and take from her. Or, the woman who dresses professionally and receives good reviews, but always has something negative to say about all the women or men in the workplace. Again, no rational reason except, I just don't like them!

Our self-esteem is not vested in our abilities. Our self-esteem must come from the Word! Every person on this planet should believe they are of high quality, not because of a degree or promotion, but because our heavenly Father designed us this way. Money, physical features, homes, relationships, and careers will come and go, but our trust in Him allows us to continually love ourselves regardless of our current circumstances.

> God said you are valuable and of high quality.

Your confidence is intertwined within your relationship with Christ. When you trust His abilities and love for you, then watch how your posture changes when you walk into a room. Watch how others feel confident in your presence because Christ lives in you. Watch how you desire less of what others have because you recognize how great you already are.

Do you know the difference between confidence and arrogance? I think the difference is honesty. A confident Christian knows God is in control and has provided gifts, talents, paths, and an abundance of ways to navigate this life. They are confident through Christ and able to spread inspiration anywhere they go. They want others to shine because they know they shine as well. They are not concerned about comparison, because they're confident in completing their own race. They know they serve a God who loves them just as much as He loves you. There is no competition in their life because none is required since their confidence is sustained through Christ.

On the other hand, an arrogant person believes everything they have accumulated, mastered, and accomplished was all done by their own abilities (and they have no problem letting everyone know). It is dangerous to be arrogant because the very definition states an "exaggeration of abilities." Arrogant people cannot be honest with themselves, because they would have to admit they are human and need help like the rest of us normal folks. They would have to admit they have no superpowers and all the education in the world is not why they have a great job. In my opinion, some arrogant people do not recognize they are the *created* and not the *Creator*.

PSALM 27:10-14 (NLT):
> *Even if my father and mother abandon me, the LORD will hold me close.* **Teach me how to live,** *O LORD. Lead me along the right path, for my enemies are waiting for me. Do not let me fall into their hands. For they accuse me of things I've never done; with every breath they threaten me with violence. Yet I am* **confident** *I will see the LORD's goodness while I am here in the land of the living. Wait patiently for the LORD.* **Be brave** *and* **courageous.** *Yes, wait patiently for the LORD.* (Emphasis mine)

Exercise 3.3: Review any highlighted notes and then respond to the section below. Are you confident or arrogant?
1. List a few things that make you feel proud of yourself.

2. List a few things you have accomplished that deserve more credit than you've given yourself (without comparing to other's accomplishments).

3. List a few things you have obtained that are deserving of more praise to God, since you didn't obtain them on your own (things you may have been a little arrogant about). Pray for forgiveness and thank God for sharing His talents with you.

Chapter 4

Deliberately Faithful:

Learning His Faithfulness

Wow, isn't God good! How wonderful to have a Lord who displays confidence and humility at the same time. So far, we have defined deliberate, discussed the *her* in your life, and learned how to be confident. Now, it is time to discuss God's faithfulness. I know you may be wondering how we can incorporate God's faithfulness into being *Deliberately Me*, but that's just it; everything about God gets us closer to being deliberate about ourselves.

We serve a God who is very deliberate in everything He does since the beginning of time. Have you ever thought about God in this way?

GENESIS 1:1-19 (NIV):

In the beginning God created the heavens and the earth. Now the earth was formless and empty, darkness was over the surface of the deep, and the Spirit of God was hovering over the waters.

And God said, *"**Let there be light**,"* *and there was light. God saw that the light **was good**, and he separated the light from the darkness. God called the light "day," and the darkness he called "night." And there was evening, and there was morning—the first day.*

And God said, *"**Let there be a vault** between the waters to separate water from water." So God made the vault and separated the water under the vault from the water above it. And it was so. God called the vault "sky." And there was evening, and there was morning—the second day.*

And God said, *"**Let the water under the sky be gathered** to one place, and let dry ground appear." And it was so. God called the dry ground "land," and the gathered waters he called "seas." And God saw that it was good. Then God said, "**Let the land produce** vegetation: seed-bearing plants and trees on the land that bear fruit with seed in it, according to their various kinds." And it was so. The land produced vegetation: plants bearing seed according to their kinds and trees bearing fruit with seed in it according to their kinds. And God saw that it was good. And there was evening, and there was morning—the third day.*

And God said, *"**Let there be lights in the vault** of the sky to separate the day from the night and let them serve as signs to mark sacred times, and days and years, and let them be lights in the vault of the sky to give light on the earth." And it was so. God made two great lights—the greater light to govern the day and the lesser light to govern the night. He also made the stars. God set them in the vault of the sky to give light on the earth, to govern the day and the night, and*

*to separate light from darkness. And God saw
that it was good. And there was evening, and
there was morning—the fourth day.* (Emphasis
mine)

The list of God's intentions (deliberate nature) goes on through
the book of Revelation into present day. Everything He did in
Genesis was a method of being deliberate—from taking six days
to create the earth, man, and even resting on the seventh day.
Through God's deliberate nature, His faithfulness is always
present.

Exercise 4.1: Read Genesis chapters one and two. How do they
pertain to your life?

_____

_____

_____

_____

_____

_____

_____

Our Lord did not create you because He was bored and wanted
something to do. God created you to be in relationship with Him.
Our God would never create something, if He didn't plan on
being present along the journey.

A perfect example is the creation of Adam and Eve. Adam
was created by God and given
dominion over the earth. The Bible
says, *"God created a garden, trees
pleasing to the eye and for food. It
also had a river which watered the*

> Through God's deliberate
> nature, His faithfulness is
> always present.

Garden" (Genesis 2:8-10, NIV). Adam needed a companion and God created a helpmate named Eve. God not only created Adam, but He provided an environment to enable him to survive and thrive. God provided everything required for him and his wife to live peacefully within certain boundaries. They also had the best weather, since coats and snow boots for the winter were never required, nor umbrellas and raincoats for the spring and summer. There was no grass to cut, leaves to rake, or snow to shovel. They lived in paradise! *Everything they needed was provided for them even after they sinned.* Although our first earthly mother and father sinned, God still provided for them. I call this *Deliberately Faithful!*

The Bible is full of numerous stories of the faithfulness of God. No one taught Him how to be faithful because God represents faithfulness. God is referenced as Love, but He is also Faithful!

Merriam-Webster.com defines *faithful* as "having or showing true and constant support or loyalty. Deserving trust: keeping your promises or doing what you are supposed to do." Another definition shows *faithfulness* as "deserving of trust." I think it's interesting that the faithfulness of someone demands trust. Perhaps this is the reason Hebrews 11:6 (NIV) states, *"And without faith it is impossible to please God, because anyone who comes to him must believe that he exists and that he rewards those who earnestly seek him."* (Emphasis mine)

Are you able to identify the deliberate faithfulness of God in your life? I don't mean the typical things many of us say every day such as, "Thank You, God, for waking me up and protecting me as I slept." Yes, I know this is important, but I want you to dig deeper. Did He ever deny you something because in the end, it protected you? For example, as women, we tend to be angry with

God because a relationship didn't work out the way we planned. Can you recognize the faithfulness of God in keeping you from people who might have hindered you from thriving?

Throughout my life, God has shut the door on a few toxic relationships. As I've matured through Christ, I don't make it past hello sometimes because of God's faithfulness that has helped me to identify trouble before it gets out of control.

Exercise 4.2: List the ways you can identify the deliberate faithfulness of God in your life.

_____

_____

_____

_____

_____

_____

_____

God's faithfulness is not all you can have from Him; God's faithfulness comes with love, support, and provision, but it also comes with discipline, mercy, and justice. You know, the way parents should treat their children in present-day. Parents love their children and are faithful to them, but they should also be faithful to administer consequences for disobedient behavior.

God did not create Adam and Eve to leave them defenseless. God is _Deliberately Faithful_, which means He is always committed to you.

God is true, faithful, and deliberate, and He expects us to mirror His example. _"So, God created mankind in his own image, in the image of God he created them; male and female he_ *created them"* (Genesis 1:27, NIV). We are created in His image; therefore, we need to illustrate deliberate faithfulness to others.

Exercise 4.3: Thinking about the image of God brings me to a question. Without opening your Bible or using any type of sermon reference, how do you view God's image? You can use words to describe Him physically, emotionally, spiritually, or any way you feel led. This is your personal view of God.

_____

_____

_____

_____

_____

_____

_____

Exercise 4.4: Based on your description above, do you think you could fit in God's image? Are you currently illustrating these things as a follower of Christ? Why or why not?

_____

_____

_____

_____

_____

_____

_____

Allow me a moment to veer off track again. What is interesting about writing books is the author is also accountable to answer questions being asked of the reader. God has asked me many of the questions that appear throughout this book, and He has assisted in my self-awareness to work on the identified broken pieces within myself. This chapter has taken me a while to write, not because I don't understand God's faithfulness, but because I realize that understanding is not enough. His faithfulness demands our faith in Him. He is deserving of our trust. The same faithful God created us in His image. I asked you what this looks like because it's not as easy to describe as some may think.

Of course, some may assume God looks like a human, right? He has eyes, hair on his head, two legs, and two arms. He can walk, talk, and interact with creation. I could be wrong, and I am no scholar, but I don't remember the physical attributes of Jesus being as important as His actions. Jesus is our Lord poured out into flesh; so yes, He did look like us, but Jesus portrayed the ultimate image of God by His daily walk.

The Scriptures, and especially the letters from the apostle Paul, stress actions through godliness, the fruit of the Spirit, loving our neighbors, and even feeding our enemies. I am focusing on the actions because some folks in this world believe image is everything. Our true relationship with Christ (image of God) is revealed and illustrated by our actions toward ourselves and others.

For followers of Christ, a new outfit with a rude disposition is not the image of God. A friendly smile with gossipy tendencies is not the image of God. Beautiful makeup from an upscale store with a designer purse (but the inability to save money) is not the image of God. Yes, we all should look our best; I also prefer to look nice. Nonetheless, how you appear to carry yourself, is not as important as how you truly represent the image of God.

Now, let's get back to where we left off, focusing on the attribute of the deliberate faithfulness of God. I tried to grasp this concept without much success. Our heavenly Father knows we are going to mess up; and I mean mess up majorly; yet, He still supports us through it all. Whether you believe it or not, we are just like the Israelites: always asking for more and never being thankful for current provisions. They had manna but wanted steak! They already had the ultimate Creator (God) but preferred to worship a created, golden calf.

The golden calf story is an excellent representation of present-day followers. Allow me to summarize the events found in Exodus 32:1-20:

- The Israelites had a leader being led by God to keep them protected.
- Moses took too long talking with God to obtain more direction for His people, so they became impatient and melted the gold that God allowed them to take from Egypt (careless stewards) and used it to build a calf. They were impatient and tired of waiting on Moses (though in reality, they were never waiting on Moses, they were waiting on God). Then, after they were done waiting, they took the blessings of God for inappropriate usage.
- Finally, the leader returned and became angry by their disrespectful and sinful behavior, which led to severe consequences. Interesting enough—and similar to our behavior—the Israelites were mad at God as if He did something wrong!

Now, allow me to summarize the event for present Israelites (us).
- We will pray for a new car, but God takes so long (so we think); therefore, we take matters into our **own hands** by using money from our 401K plan, or obtaining a loan

with a 26% interest rate. The outcome is we end up having a car payment that is more than we can afford.

- We're tired of working at a job with mean co-workers and conclude that we need to leave the company, although we haven't discussed the situation with God yet. Regardless, we decide to go ahead with **our plan** and quit our job. Now, friends and family are subjected to our complaining of unpaid bills and we hate the new job more than the last one.

- We're tired of being lonely, so we call an ex-boyfriend, although the Lord made it very clear on numerous occasions to flee from this person. Nevertheless, we want to satisfy **our desires** over the Lord's and decide to start dating him again. Now, we're unhappy because our ex is still the same, has not matured, and still disrespects us.

- We're having constant financial struggles and ask the Lord for an increase in our finances. The Lord answers by making a way for us to have additional funds to pay off our debt. Instead of paying off the debt, **we use** the extra money for shopping and non-necessities. Now, we are stuck working two jobs instead of one.

- We are frustrated, disappointed, angry, and hurt because of our current troubles. We begin to blame God because He didn't make things clear enough for us to understand! Then, **we stop** going to church, paying our tithes, and participating in the family of God. We think we're punishing God by disconnecting from Him, but in truth, we are only hurting ourselves because **we need** Him to survive!

Some of us are very similar to the Israelites in biblical times. We tend to pray to God and He shows up, but not the way we want; so, we try to become God and make our own provisions. At some point, we cause more chaos in our world because we were impatient and more interested in feeding our desires, than becoming fed by the Spirit. Does this sound about right? I still struggle with this and God reminded me of Galatians 5.

GALATIANS 5:13:21 (NIV):

> *You, my brothers and sisters, were called to be free. But do not use your freedom to indulge the flesh; rather, serve one another humbly in love. For the entire law is fulfilled in keeping this one command: "Love your neighbor as yourself." If you bite and devour each other, watch out or you will be destroyed by each other.*
>
> ***So, I say, walk by the Spirit, and you will not gratify the desires of the flesh. For the flesh desires what is contrary to the Spirit, and the Spirit what is contrary to the flesh. They are in conflict with each other, so that you are not to do whatever you want.*** *But if you are led by the Spirit, you are not under the law.*
>
> *The acts of the flesh are obvious: sexual immorality, impurity and debauchery; idolatry and witchcraft; hatred, discord, jealousy, fits of rage, selfish ambition, dissensions, factions and envy; drunkenness, orgies, and the like. I warn you, as I did before, that those who live like this will not inherit the kingdom of God. (Emphasis mine)*

God was and still is faithful to us, even when we blatantly (intentionally) ignore His commands. How many times has God saved you from the mess you created? Better yet, how many times will God have to keep saving you from your creation of chaos (not the adversary)? I know we like to blame the devil for many things, but now is the time to be honest. How many times did things become worse because you were stubborn, impatient, uneducated on a matter, or confident in your own abilities?

Exercise 4.5: Write down a few examples of self-inflicted chaos.

_____

_____

_____

_____

_____

_____

_____

Exercise 4.6: List examples of how Jesus has saved you from the self-inflicted wounds (events).

_____

_____

_____

_____

_____

_____

_____

Chapter 5

Deliberately Created:

Learning why you were created

What a faithful God we serve! I hope this book is bringing you comfort through knowing our God as an intentional Father. Everything He has completed and continues to do is an intentional act of love. Our Father has deliberately given you confidence through Christ and will always be deliberately faithful to you. He was even deliberate in creating you.

Did you know God took His time to mold your various attributes, including hair color and length, eye shape, your height, arms and legs, the way your voice sounds, and even personality traits? He created the human body and all the functions within it. Isn't it an awesome process how the heart pumps blood and muscles provide strength, while our brain can hold massive amounts of information? For those knowledgeable about computers, our brain is a human database that can store short- and long-term information. God designed us with capabilities to learn new information and the ability to retain it for years. We're able to use different methods of communication and display an array of emotions (which sometimes can get us into trouble).

By the way, don't ever forget that our Lord created you! You didn't hatch like chickens or evolve from years of changes in the ecosystem. During the time in our mother's womb, our Creator was fashioning, molding, and thrusting us into this world to become. Become what, you ask? I don't know! Your "to become" purpose is between you and God, which is why our very existence and ability to be *who we are* is because of *who He is*. Our intelligence and passion for good things are the direct result of what He instilled in us from the beginning, and it continues to work through us. Our ability to receive and give love to others is from God. The deep desire to be valued is because God Himself planted an inkling in our spirit that He loves us and so should others.

Merriam-Webster.com defines the word *creator* as "a person who makes something new." Another way of saying that is someone who "brings something into existence." What comes to your mind when you think of something new? I think of something clean, or clothing that has never been worn. Or, my new pots and pans still in the packaging, waiting to be used for a recipe I found online. When I think of a new car, I think of the leather smell and shine from the new tires and waxed exterior. When I think of new, I think of plastic or the bubble wrap I get to pop until my daughters tell me to grow up. When I think of new, I also think of what used to be and what new changes will occur: Fresh start, better outlook, or first-time experience.

Another definition identifies the word *creation* as "not existing before; made, introduced, or discovered recently or now for the first time." Is the definition trying to tell us that when something is new, it has never existed before? This should be exciting for you because there will never be another you. There was never a you until God (the Creator) created you, and there will never be another you after you have passed on. You are one of a kind!

WHAT DO THE SCRIPTURES SAY ABOUT THE CREATOR?

COLOSSIANS 1:15-16 (NLT):

Christ is the visible image of the invisible God. He existed before anything was created and is supreme over all creation, for through him God created everything in the heavenly realms and on earth. He made the things we can see and the things we can't see—such as thrones, kingdoms, rulers, and authorities in the unseen world. Everything was created through him and for him.

REVELATION 4:11 (NIV):

You are worthy, our Lord and God, to receive glory and honor and power, for you created all things, and by your will they were created and have their being.

WHAT DOES GOD SAY ABOUT HIMSELF?

ISAIAH 43:10-11 (NLT):

*"But you are my witnesses, O Israel!" says the LORD. "You are my servant. You have been chosen to know me, believe in me, and understand that **I alone am God**. There is no other God—there never has been, and there never will be. I, yes I, am the LORD, and there is no other Savior."* (Emphasis mine)

ISAIAH 45:18 (NLT):

*For the LORD is God, and he created the heavens and earth and put everything in place. He made the world to be lived in, **not to be a place of empty chaos**. "I am the LORD," he says, "and there is no other."* (Emphasis mine)

ISAIAH 66:2 (NIV):

"Has not my hand made all these things, and so they came into being?" declares the LORD.

Notice how the Lord tells us *"He alone"* is God. This is good news for His creation because Scripture says He will always be present. We the *created* can be assured God will never make plans to take a vacation from playing an active role in our lives.

PSALM 139:1-24 (NKJV):

O LORD, You have searched me and known me. You know my sitting down and my rising up; You understand my thought afar off. You comprehend my path and my lying down and are acquainted with all my ways. For there is not a word on my tongue, but behold, O LORD, You know it altogether. You have hedged me behind and before and laid Your hand upon me. Such knowledge is too wonderful for me; It is high, I cannot attain it.

Where can I go from Your Spirit? Or where can I flee from Your presence? If I ascend into heaven, You are there; If I make my bed in hell, behold, You are there. If I take the wings of the morning, and dwell in the uttermost parts of the sea, even there Your hand shall lead me, and Your right hand shall hold me. If I say, "Surely the darkness shall fall on me," even the night shall be light about me; Indeed, the darkness shall not hide from You, but the night shines as the day; The darkness and the light are both alike to You.

For You formed my inward parts; You covered me in my mother's womb. I will praise You, for I am fearfully and wonderfully made; Marvelous are Your works, and that my soul knows very well. *My frame was not hidden from You, when I was made in secret, and skillfully wrought in the lowest parts of the earth. Your eyes saw my substance, being yet unformed. And in Your book, they all were written, The days fashioned for me, When as yet there were none of them.*

How precious also are Your thoughts to me, O God! How great is the sum of them? If I should count them, they would be more in number than the sand; When I awake, I am still with You.

Oh, that You would slay the wicked, O God! Depart from me, therefore, you bloodthirsty men. For they speak against You wickedly; Your enemies take Your name in vain. Do I not hate them, O LORD, who hate You? And do I not loathe those who rise up against You? I hate them with perfect hatred; I count them my enemies.

Search me, O God, and know my heart; Try me, and know my anxieties; And see if there is any wicked way in me and lead me in the way everlasting. (Emphasis mine)

WHAT DOES GOD SAY ABOUT HIS CREATION?

PHILIPPIANS 1:6 (NIV):
. . .being confident of this, that he who began a good work in you will carry it on to completion until the day of Christ Jesus.

This Scripture leads me to another question. How many times have you started something and given up in the beginning, halfway through, or even right before the finish? How did this make you feel? Perhaps a thought you should take away from Philippians 1:6 is that God's continued work will never be dependent on your strength; however, it is dependent on your faith in Him to believe He can help you finish the work.

What I am trying to convey is your projects, career, hobbies, and daily activities are things you desire to complete. You decided to plant a garden but now have other areas requiring your attention and find it impossible to get everything planted. The garden is your goal, being done in your natural human strength. God's plan for us is not dependent on our natural human strength nor our understanding. It only requires us to believe He created us in His image; He sent Jesus to die for us and, by faith and repentance, we have a relationship with Him, which allows Him to continually work in and through us.

GENESIS 1:26-28 (NKJV):

> Then God said, "Let Us make man in Our image, according to Our likeness; let them have dominion over the fish of the sea, over the birds of the air, and over the cattle, over all the earth and over every creeping thing that creeps on the earth." So God created man in His own image; in the image of God He created him; male and female He created them. Then God blessed them, and God said to them, "**Be fruitful** and **multiply**; fill the earth and **subdue** it; **have dominion** over the fish of the sea, over the birds of the air, and over every living thing that moves on the earth." (Emphasis mine)

GENESIS 1:26-28 (MSG):

*God spoke: "Let us make human beings in our image, make them reflecting our nature, so they can be responsible for the fish in the sea, the birds in the air, the cattle, And, yes, Earth itself, and every animal that moves on the face of Earth." God created human beings; he created them godlike, Reflecting God's nature. He created them male and female. God blessed them: "**Prosper! Reproduce! Fill Earth! Take charge!** Be responsible for fish in the sea and birds in the air, for every living thing that moves on the face of Earth."* (Emphasis mine)

Can you grasp the instructions placed upon God's creation? The New King James translation says for male and female to "Be fruitful, multiply, subdue and have dominion" (v. 28). God deliberately created every single one of us with a purpose and He made it quite simple. I also listed a second translation to highlight the importance for these instructions. God deliberately created us to "Prosper! Reproduce! Fill Earth! Take charge!" (v. 28). You and I were deliberately created to do all these things!

PROSPER!

Exercise 5.1: What do you think of God's instruction for us to prosper?

_____

_____

_____

_____

_____

For some, prosper means the ability to obtain heaps of money and other stuff. For others, it may mean popularity among certain groups, or an achievement by growing in your career. Possibly these are means for prospering, but where does this leave those who lack money, material items, or the impressive executive title at the office? We could be sending the wrong message that prospering is about *obtainment* and less about the *ability to produce* (bring forth). For this reason, I decided to use a definition found on Merriam-Webster.com: "to cause to succeed or thrive." The Bible talks about prospering, but the Genesis Scriptures are not about increasing your net value, your bank account, or how many trips you can take annually.

The apostle Paul talked about prospering, succeeding, and thriving. But, his version of prospering is *through* Christ, not titles or by accumulating large sums of material items.

Paul even said you can prosper regardless of your finances, shelter arrangements, and career status. He learned to live in need and with plenty, but an important lesson he taught us is to be content in any situation (Philippians 4:11-12). He could do all of this and prosper through Christ.

Another way to understand Paul's emphasis about prospering is to grow *with* Christ. Some of the letters he wrote dealt with our commitment to Christ and love for others, in addition to the treatment and commitment of our gifts and involvement in the Body (the Church). Yes, I said treatment because many of us are not good stewards of our gifts. We use them for manipulation instead of exaltation or exhortation of others.

How do you know you are prospering through Christ? You know by experiencing fruits of all kinds in your walk. You know by your relationship growth with the Lord and growth in wisdom (Psalm 1:3, Luke 9:23-27, James 3:17). Prosperity does mean some type of growth, but from a spiritual perspective, this doesn't necessarily mean an abundance of cash flow. Spiritual fruit is constant, steady, enrichment of yourself and others. Paul states in Romans 12:9 (NIV): *"Love must be sincere. Hate what is evil; cling to what is good."*

Are you prospering in love? Are you prospering by *"not becoming overcome by evil but overcoming evil with good,"* as instructed in Romans 12:21 (NIV)? No follower of Christ is prospering if their relationship is not prospering through Christ. Our total dependence for spiritual prosperity (succeeding and thriving) is through Christ. So, how do we identify what true prosperity looks like?

MARK 12:29-31 (NLT):
> *Jesus replied, "The most important commandment is this: 'Listen, O Israel! The LORD our God is the one and only LORD. And you must* **love the LORD** *your God with all your heart, all your soul, all your mind, and all your strength.' The second is equally important:* **'Love your neighbor** *as yourself.' No other commandment is greater than these."* (Emphasis mine)

A few ways to do this is by:

- Becoming a mentor for **empowering, encouraging,** and **building** up others.
- Having a **willingness** to help others on their job (even when they're not the friendliest co-worker).
- Being a **peacemaker** between individuals or even groups of people.

- Being a parent willing to **evolve** and **listen** to your children, instead of being a tyrant.
- **Extending grace** in your marriage by not always expecting your husband to do things your way.
- Treating everyone **respectfully**, regardless of their behavior toward you.
- Learning that sometimes **silence**— *"to cause to cease hostile firing or criticism"* —is just as much a virtue as patience.

So, my sister, you are called to prosper through Christ! Prosper by giving your all to Him, the one who gave His one and only begotten Son to us. Prosper by loving yourself because God loves you and wants you to prosper by duplicating the same love to others. The goal is not to be perfect but to learn from your mistakes, prosper, and do better the next time.

REPRODUCE!

Exercise 5.2: What do you think of God's instruction for us to reproduce?

_____

_____

_____

_____

_____

_____

_____

Regardless of what someone may have told you or tried to speak over you, *everyone* can reproduce something. Reproducing doesn't mean that every woman is going to bare or raise children, but it does mean all of us have the gift to bring something to life. Have you taken a failed project and applied your gifts, creating something new, usable, and beneficial for someone else? Were you able to take a simple idea and do great things because of it? Have your ideas and efforts blessed others to evolve into something greater?

Dictionary.com has a definition of the word *reproduce* that I especially like: "to make a copy, representation, duplicate, or close imitation of; to reproduce a picture." In a way, this reminds me of the Great Commission.

MATTHEW 28:16-20 (NKJV):

> *Then the eleven disciples went away into Galilee, to the mountain which Jesus had appointed for them. When they saw Him, they worshiped Him; but some doubted. And Jesus came and spoke to them, saying, "All authority has been given to Me in heaven and on earth.* **Go therefore and make disciples of all the nations,** *baptizing them in the name of the Father and of the Son and of the Holy Spirit,* **teaching them to observe all things that I have commanded you;** *and lo, I am with you always, even to the end of the age." Amen.* (Emphasis mine)

Jesus was instructing His disciples (and us, too) to "duplicate/copy," to reproduce His work. Jesus was asking them to go out and make more disciples who would also follow His commands.

Based on Matthew 28, all of us can follow the commands of Jesus, and then *reproduce* those efforts in various areas. I will use a phrase mentioned a lot at my place of employment: "Think outside the box." Many of you only use your gifts at church, home, or for special occasions. If this is the case for you, how are you reproducing if your gifts are limited to one location, one group, and special occasions? This type of practice reminds me of the quote for insanity, which is "doing the same thing over and over and expecting a different result." Now, I am not saying to stop producing where you are, but remember, Jesus sent his disciples *out* to reproduce! Reproducing requires more than staying in our comfort zone; it requires being around others who don't look, think, act, or even speak the same language.

Reproducing requires courage so that you can be used anywhere at any time. Yes, that last sentence is a little scary. It scared me when I wrote it! It requires the willingness to share our gifts with more than just those close to us. It requires us to share outside of those we trust and even those outside of our cliques.

Some of you may still be wondering what are some ways to reproduce? You and I need to be praying how to circulate our gifts through all channels. We need to be praying and asking the Lord are we at the place He has called us to be? Are we in a position to be connected to those who will benefit and assist in God's will, or are we becoming stagnant in our reproduction?

Some of you may be thinking, I have no idea what this author just said. Maybe you're thinking you have never created or produced anything, but I bet you have.

One of my favorite saying is "don't make this harder than it really is." Follow whatever God has laid on your heart and commit to doing this in every area of your life. I am sure God wants the good in you to be visible to all. Don't limit His gifts to just one place. If He asks you to go, then go! If He asks you to stay, then stay! Just don't stop reproducing!

If you're still confused by what reproduction really means for you, allow the passage on the following page to encourage you that God wants to know your plans. He wants to be involved in directing and assisting you with reproducing.

PSALM 37:3-5 (NLT):

*Trust in the LORD and do good. Then you will live safely in the land and prosper. Take delight in the LORD, and he will give you your heart's desires. **Commit everything you do to the LORD.** Trust him, and he will help you.* (Emphasis mine)

When I first read verse four of the above passage, I was so excited to be a Christian because the NKJV version says, *"And He shall give you the desires of your heart."* In my mind, this meant that if I am happy with God, then He would give me everything I want, right? What a good God we serve! No! This is *not* what the Scripture means! When you are reading the Word, spending time with God and time alone meditating to hear from God, you will begin to perceive God's heart. You will hear what He designed and gifted you to be. You will begin to hear this louder than your own desires. Then, you will know it is God because it is usually something you would have never thought for yourself (and this desire will positively haunt you until your purpose is activated).

Reproduction doesn't require a pastor of a mega church or a well-known inspirational Christian speaker, but it does require a heart submissive to

> Trust in the Lord and do good.

God's will. The fact you have chosen to read this book is not because I desired to become an author. You are reading this book because this is one of God's desires for me, to help beautiful women like you in being deliberate in everything you do. Therefore, delight in the Lord and reproduce!

FILL THE EARTH!

Exercise 5.3: What does this phrase mean to you?

_____

_____

_____

_____

_____

_____

We have managed to fill the earth with pollution, cell phones, gas-guzzling cars, and landfills. In addition, the world is filled with an unhealthy usage of social media outlets, which have led folks to increased depression, bitterness, and low self-esteem. We have filled this world with more technology than the human mind can process.

We have also filled the earth with some beautiful things, such as Breyers® Blasts! Oreo Cookies & Cream Chocolate ice cream, Adam's® Peanut Butter Cup Fudge Ripple Cheesecake, barkTHINS® snacking chocolate, and Reese's® Peanut Butter Cups. Don't judge. . .you have your list of good things and I have mine. Nevertheless, I think we can agree the world is filled with things.

What comes to mind when you think of filling something up? I instantly think of another cup of coffee, a bowl of Lucky Charms™ cereal, or two more cookies on my plate, although I probably should use an educational source. One definition from Dictionary.com for the word _fill_ means "to occupy to the full capacity, to be plentiful throughout, or enough to satisfy or desire." Two suggested synonyms for the word _plentiful_ are abundance and overflowing. Based on the synonyms, is God telling us to *overflow* throughout this world?

GALATIANS 5:22-23 (NIV):

But the fruit of the Spirit is love, joy, peace, forbearance, kindness, goodness, faithfulness, gentleness, self-control. Against such things there is no law.

What better way to fill the earth than by spreading love, peace, and joy. Because of Christ, we have been empowered through the Holy Spirit to spread healthy fruit, which can be eaten and absorbed by believers and unbelievers. You were deliberately created to be in relationship with God and others. The only way to be in godly relationships the way our heavenly Father intended is by exhibiting the fruit of the Spirit. Today the world is in chaos because some followers of Jesus are displaying the adversary's behaviors (sexual immorality, debauchery, idolatry, hatred, discord, jealousy, rage, self-ambition, listed in Galatians 5:19-21), rather than those of Christ, listed in Galatians 5:22-23.

At times, followers begin to experience spiritual dementia (memory loss) and they forget who is their true Helper. Perhaps they have forgotten because they no longer experience certain struggles. They have forgotten because God is so faithful. They have forgotten because God has placed them in a position to help but they would rather use their money, time, and gifts on other things. Even worse, some have been given leadership positions that have caused them to have very high and mighty opinions of themselves. Unfortunately, these are fruitless examples that can turn a humble, gentle Christian into an arrogant, prideful destroyer.

When the Lord commanded us to "fill the earth," He didn't mean to fill it with lies, adultery, malice, fear, worry, envy, unhealthy competition, and gossip. God meant for us to fill the earth with the fruit of the Spirit. The only way to do this is if every Christian is using their gifts for good. The only way to fill this entire world with Christ-like ways is to always illustrate His love, peace, joy, kindness, goodness, gentleness, self-control, forbearance, and faithfulness.

How many times have you heard someone through prayer request God to "fill this place"? They are asking for God's presence to come. In return, we should illustrate His presence everywhere we go. How do you plan to go forth and fill this place? We must overflow this earth with God's love, which is what He did for us through the sacrificial act of Jesus Christ.

TAKE CHARGE!

So far, we've learned to Prosper, Reproduce, and Fill the Earth; lastly, we'll discuss how to Take Charge. But, take charge of what? Yes, I know God mentioned some birds and fish. But does He really mean we should tell the birds and fish what to do? If so, I wish my cat Izzie listened more when I take charge. No matter how many times I say no, she still sneaks onto my couch to sleep. Perhaps cats were not part of the deal for taking charge of their lives.

I think I do a good job of bossing my kids around or letting people know when they have upset me. Is this what God meant when He said, "Take Charge?"

Exercise 5.4: What do you think it means to Take Charge?

_____

_____

_____

_____

_____

_____

_____

Now that you have written your examples, let me provide another Scripture from 2 Timothy 1:7 (KJV): _"For God hath not given us the spirit of fear; but of power, and of love, and of a sound mind."_

Many of us relate to the above verse, especially when we are dealing with things that mess with our thought process, things that make us feel like we are going crazy, or chaos that has us wondering where God is, and does He really love us. We look to this Scripture because we may be feeling anxious or afraid something will happen, or maybe something has happened, and we don't know the next step to remediate the problem. Maybe, just maybe, we feel totally powerless against this thing that is troubling us. Maybe we don't even feel like loving and treating others the way Jesus commanded, because of this heavy burden keeping us up at night.

And, now a brief pause for a moment of rambling.

As I write this book at eight o'clock at night, I am dealing with the what's next in my life and where does God want me to go. I am experiencing fear of the unknown and anxiety about the future. I am also dealing with a control problem in thinking, _"I should know how to handle what's next,"_ but I don't (and that is okay). Followers of Christ, we will not always have an exact plan of what to do or where to go, but we can trust the Lord to have the full plan, resources, and commitment to get us to our what's next.

Are you still pondering what "take charge" means? It means exactly what 2 Timothy 1:7 states. Reading and meditating on this is the easy part. Taking charge means you believe that Jesus Christ died for you, and that you have a confident, victorious spirit. You demonstrate the active faith and power that Jesus Christ lives in you.

2 TIMOTHY 1:7-14 (MSG):

God doesn't want us to be shy with His gifts, *but bold and loving and sensible.*

So don't be embarrassed to speak up for our Master or for me, his prisoner. Take your share of suffering for the Message along with the rest of us. *We can only keep on going, after all, by the power of God*, *who first saved us and then* *called us to this holy work*. *We had nothing to do with it. It was all his idea, a gift prepared for us in Jesus long before we knew anything about it. But we know it now. Since the appearance of our Savior, nothing could be plainer: death defeated, life vindicated in a steady blaze of light, all through the work of Jesus.*

This is the Message I've been set apart to proclaim as preacher, emissary, and teacher. It's also the cause of all this trouble I'm in. But I have no regrets. I couldn't be more sure of my ground—the One I've trusted in can take

*care of what he's trusted me to do right to
the end.*

*So keep at your work, this faith and love rooted
in Christ, exactly as I set it out for you. It's as
sound as the day you first heard it from me.*
**Guard this precious thing placed in your
custody by the Holy Spirit who works in
us**. (Emphasis mine)

If you didn't grab some nuggets from Paul for taking charge, then
stop reading this book right now because this is all I've got (just
joking). Paul is letting us know he experienced challenges, due to
his choice to live for Christ by choosing to spread a message to all
believers.

To take charge was never about being abusive or bossy,
but God knew one day His children would have to take a stand.
This stand is either for Christ or for everything else. When you
stand for Christ, you must take charge because trials, dry spells,
and worldly chaos won't stop until our Savior returns. The good
news is you have been equipped with gifts to help yourself and
others make it through another day. It also means you are going
to have to deal with many people who don't agree with your
beliefs; but there's no need for worry, because we don't have to
be afraid nor ashamed of what Jesus did for all of us.

The Lord already knew His people were going to be faced
with hard choices, yet God in the beginning told Adam and Eve
to take charge. You need to remember the only true ruler is the
Lord. He is the only One to whom we surrender all we have.
Doing so allows us to take charge over the life we have through
Christ. If you are aware of your gifts, don't be shy or concerned
about what others think. Take charge and be a wise steward over
the areas the Lord has given you! Whatever God has blessed you

to have and lead, take charge and lead others in a path of righteousness by using your gifts and resources. Don't wait for when you're ready, when God has already given you everything you need.

Chapter 6

Deliberately Me:

Learning to be You on purpose with purpose

This chapter is all about being you on purpose; the reason you get to be you! We have discussed the reasons throughout this entire book for *why* it is okay to just be you. I also hope you are learning God purposely created you to be just the way you are. Matter of fact, the definition of the word *purpose* according to Dictionary.com is "the reason for which something exists or is done, made, and used; an intended or desired result, aim or goal."

Does this mean that when God created you, He had a goal or intended result in mind? Do you understand that you right now are an intended result? We talked about being *Deliberately Created* in the last chapter, but this seals the deal. Of course, this doesn't suggest that the you today are in the final stage of growth; but it does mean there is something God intended to happen to and for you. There are certain things about you that are always going to make others either uncomfortable or drawn toward you. This is okay since it was God's original plan from the beginning.

It is not your role or plan to figure out *the how* for getting people to like you, but it is your job to figure out *the how* in utilizing your God-given personality and gifts to benefit the Kingdom.

I know this may sound like a cliché, especially if you attend church, watch online services, or listen to Christian radio, but you have been empowered with an abundance of spiritual knowledge, gifts, talents, and free will to impact God's people in a positive or negative way. It is your choice whether you will allow the Holy Spirit to shape you along the way. To be shaped, you'll need time with God for continual guidance to stay near the path. I state *near* the path because we are not always going to get it right, and the Lord knows this. Unfortunately, no one has the right formula, but I've chosen to share a few insights to assist you in being the best *Deliberately You*.

The purpose of the following sections is to share some thoughts on how the Lord crafted women for various reasons. Perhaps you may identify with some or all the sections. The overall goal is for you to be okay in knowing God deliberately created you just the way you are!

DELIBERATELY ME #1
THE GREAT LISTENER

If you're this type of person, you probably speak to everyone no matter where you go or who is with you. You are intrigued by meeting new people and are a social butterfly (at times). You can start up conversations while in the line at the store, waiting for your delayed flight at the airport, or even the restroom. Total strangers share personal stories about their wayward children or their sister's second battle with cancer. Some people are just drawn to you because of *what* God has put in you. What is *the what* about you? Possibly it is the way you smile, or your approachable demeanor, or your tendency to demonstrate joy. In this world, we will forever need drops of joy—a smile or two for the faint-hearted in the grocery line, the single mom whose toddler won't stop screaming, the stranger jogging who received news he has cancer, or the co-worker whose brother died.

You were not created this way by mistake or out of boredom. What's so interesting about God's supernatural intention for us, is it doesn't require a Bachelor's or Master's degree. You are gifted (through Christ) to encourage, uplift, speak highly, and overthrow all negative intentions coming toward God's people. At times, it may feel like your joy and happiness are dependent on the joy of others. I am not implying you are only happy through others, but I am saying uplifting people brings you joy. It is a passion of yours to provide a Word to those you love or strangers you just met. You want them happy, motivated, and not quitting their race. You are deliberately and uniquely gifted to exhort, encourage, and motivate others. This was not by mistake but done for an "intended result" to love your neighbor, which glorifies God.

At times, I am sure you face some opposition with others or difficulties in being you. You probably are the listener in most relationships. This means you do 90% of the listening and everyone else does 90% of the talking. Matter of fact, I don't know too many of your kind without the ability to listen. At times, you may be the go-to person for other peoples' troubles; and every so often, you might get a sentence or two in when you're going through something. As a result of being created this way, you can go long periods as a support for others. Friends, family, and co-workers always share their problems. They may ask about yours, but it's more of a courtesy rather than an invitation to share.

Nonetheless, you are okay with this because God has provided you the required amount of grace and passion to help your brothers and sisters.

You're probably wondering what any of this has to do with being *Deliberately You?* How can I be *Deliberately Me,* when I am always deliberately listening to someone else's problems? How am I learning to be me on purpose by listening to others all the time?

I must say I thought the ending of this book was going to be about this as well, but God has a funny way of changing our plans. The bottom line is you were never intended to focus on you all the time; you were never intended to be caught up with your own problems. No child of God should be. You were deliberately and spiritually ordained by God to bring joy and "the what" about you at all times. The Bible mentions the word *joy* at least 150 times (depending on the translation), and without joy in the world, it would be far worse than it is now. You were gifted through Christ to be a person of encouragement, which also means you will have to deal with people like Debbie Downer, Negative Nancy, Rude Regina, and Woe-is-Me Wilma.

Just remember, you don't have to apologize for being you, and don't be dismayed for those you can't change. It was never meant for you to change or save anyone. You are the messenger of the Good News, and Jesus Christ is the Savior.

2 CORINTHIANS 1:3-7 (NLT):

> *All praise to God, the Father of our Lord Jesus Christ. God is our merciful Father and the source of all comfort.* **He comforts us in all our troubles so that we can comfort others. When they are troubled, we will be able to give them the same comfort God has given**

us. *For the more we suffer for Christ, the more God will shower us with his comfort through Christ. Even when we are weighed down with troubles, it is for your comfort and salvation! For when we ourselves are comforted, we will certainly comfort you. Then you can patiently endure the same things we suffer. We are confident that as you share in our sufferings, you will also share in the comfort God gives us.* (Emphasis mine)

Your intended purpose (and not your only purpose) is to uplift, inspire, and catapult others forward! So, please encourage by any means necessary through love. Love is a great sacrifice, which means at times you must be inconsiderate to yourself in order to be courteous to others; therefore, seek God for comfort, grace, and strength to refill your encouragement tank when it is low. Seriously! Having gifts doesn't mean you always find joy in using them, which is why we need Jesus for a constant refill of His love in order to continue spreading love.

DELIBERATELY ME #2
THE HUMBLE WORKER

Desire to serve is another type of intended purpose. If you're this type of person, you see the need and contemplate various ways to help others. More importantly, you are not concerned with recognition, but for the mission and overall success of the endeavor.

If this is you, then you may be an avid volunteer within or outside your community. Remember, a volunteer doesn't have to be on a committee or belong to a local non-profit organization. Your purpose allows you to help in various ways without being limited to just one group. You enjoy helping; and sometimes without thinking, you just say yes. You don't mind serving others regardless of their status (homeless or political official). You don't mind cleaning floors of the church or packing bags at the pantry. You were gifted to do what others refuse to do and because of this, you may encounter those who look down on you. You have chosen to be around people from all walks of life: homeless, children in poverty, or even drug addicts. Possibly you've chosen a lower paying job because your passion is to help others in their area of lack. You don't mind donating clothes for those in need or spending your money to feed a family. Your intended purpose allows you to only see the need and not the color or status of a person.

COLOSSIANS 3:23-24 (NIV):

Whatever you do, work at it with all your heart, as working for the Lord, not for human masters, since you know that you will receive an inheritance from the Lord as a reward. It is the Lord Christ you are serving.

Let me remind you, this desire you have was deliberately instilled in you. Though you probably go unnoticed by others, God notices you. He notices the yards you mow and the houses you clean. He notices the older couple next door you check on periodically and the cat food you provide for the strays. He notices the various countries you traveled to for helping the poor and students you've tutored. He notices you are the first to arrive and the last to leave to ensure things are in order. He notices your faithfulness to the leaders in the church and the elders requiring assistance. He notices your faithfulness as a volunteer at your job and the children's school.

God already knew how dedicated you would be because He deliberately gifted you this way. One of your intended results is the capacity to assist with the needs of various people; therefore, continue to deliberately serve in all capacities. Don't allow the utterings of others to stop God's work through you. The Lord's will is being done through your serving, and this is what matters most.

DELIBERATELY ME #3
FRIENDLY FOLKS

Do you know any friendly folks? You've probably been to their house multiple times and continue to go because you feel right at home. Perhaps you're the friendly person, always inviting people over or even out for a fun event. I don't think all friendly folks invite people into their home, but they do have a knack for making you feel welcomed regardless of where you are. They might even be talented in cooking, games, crafts, event planning, knitting, entertaining (great sense of humor), and much more. Sometimes they're the first to suggest meeting at their home but the last to eat (since they're serving everyone else).

Friendly folks enjoy making everyone comfortable and meeting the needs of the people in the room. Have you ever noticed how thoughtful they are in planning events for their audience so that everyone has a good time? Although we are human and can never be 100% satisfied, people with this desire will always try to make their guests feel 100% content. They genuinely care about the well-being, likes, and dislikes of other people.

Friendly folks are the type of people who make mental notes. If you mention a preference for chocolate cake (hint, hint), then chocolate cake will probably be at the next gathering. (We may not live in the same city, but my favorite dessert *is* chocolate cake, and I would love if you would invite me over sometime.)

I think friendly folks are awesome, especially since I don't enjoy cooking and cleaning, and suffer from the inability to hide my frustration over spilled food on the floors and counter tops. Sorry for getting derailed for a moment; the last comment was supposed to be a silent thought, but I know some of you will agree with me.

On the flip side, if you have been identified as friendly, then, sadly, some may think you're a busybody; but you can't help it.

LUKE 10:38-42 (NKJV):

Now it happened as they went that He entered a certain village; and a certain woman named Martha welcomed Him into her house. And she had a sister called Mary, who also sat at Jesus' feet and heard His word. But Martha was distracted with much serving, and she approached Him and said, "Lord, do You not care that my sister has left me to serve alone? Therefore, tell her to help me." And Jesus answered and said to her, "Martha, Martha, you are worried and troubled about many things, but one thing is needed, and Mary has chosen that good part, which will not be taken away from her."

I wonder if Martha had this desire because she was more focused on the turkey in the oven and burning the gravy on the stove than sitting with Jesus. I'm just joking, but we all know the intent of the Scripture. Friendly folks are gifted to provide a comfortable and loving environment.

It may bother you at times if you have this gift and have been called a busybody. I would encourage you that time spent with God is important. It is the only way to utilize your gifts the way they were intended. You will overload yourself doing a lot of busy work instead of the will of God. This ability is nothing to be ashamed of, so don't stop making people comfortable and showing concern for entertaining others. You were given this desire *on purpose* to meet the needs of God's people. You were given this gift to help others feel safe, secure, and, at times, vulnerable to communicate real issues instead of the phrase, "I'm fine." Your genuine care for others is obvious by all the things you are committed to doing (through Christ) for His people.

HEBREWS 13:1-3 (MSG):

> *Stay on good terms with each other, held together by love. Be ready with a meal or a bed when it's needed. Why, some have extended hospitality to angels without ever knowing it! Regard prisoners as if you were in prison with them. Look on victims of abuse as if what happened to them had happened to you.*

Of course, there are more Scriptures illustrating love toward others, which is why you shouldn't be afraid to imitate Jesus when everyone else is too busy.

DELIBERATELY ME #4
THE SYMPATHETIC HEART

Isn't it intriguing how God *Deliberately Created* so many unique individuals? We have the great listeners, humble workers, friendly folks, and now let's discuss the sympathetic hearts.

These followers have grasped the message of Proverbs 15:1 (AMP):*"A soft and gentle and thoughtful answer turns away wrath, but harsh and painful and careless words stir up anger."* I've met a few people with this superpower (or shall I say, the ability to listen first before blurting out a response). These folks are self-aware, full of wisdom, and know how to forgive others rather than illustrating the typical, judgmental behavior.

These folks have more patience than the average human and are very empathetic toward God's people facing various situations. These folks remind me of Jesus in how He can see past the sinful nature and offer help in the midst of our brokenness. Sometimes a simple, listening ear or friendly reminder that we were all sinners can make a huge difference in the lives of others.

If this is you, you may find yourself reminding those struggling in their walk that God loves them regardless of their sins. You are in-tune with the Lord's hurting children and aim to help alleviate their pain. You would rather show compassion than point the finger and degrade someone. You may even be more level-headed than most in difficult situations. Please do not use the last sentence to win an argument about being rational with your husband or close friend. Occasionally, even the most empathetic, compassionate, and level-headed person can lack wisdom in certain situations.

Perhaps you are a good mediator because it is important to you for everyone's side/version/voice to be heard. As mentioned in chapter one, compassion is necessary because an absence of compassion results in indifference, cruelty, and exclusion. Therefore, I reiterate, if this is you, you are needed.

Your purpose of spreading a sympathetic heart to the people of God is essential. The world will always be filled with broken and downtrodden people. This world is also filled with an enormous number of proud folks—folks too busy with their own problems to sympathize with others and with no clue what the word *empathy* even means. Or, folks who feel "they" should have known better, so why waste my time? Because of proud people, more of the wise, merciful, and empathetic children of God are needed.

> An absence of compassion, results in indifference, cruelty, and exclusion.

If this is you, please continue to care and support your sisters and brothers (even those who don't know Jesus yet). We need your willingness to be present by showing the character of Jesus when no one else will.

ROMANS 3:22-24 (NIV):

This righteousness is given through faith in Jesus Christ to all who believe. There is no difference between Jew and Gentile, for all have sinned and fall short of the glory of God, and all are justified freely by his grace through the redemption that came by Christ Jesus.

DELIBERATELY ME #5
THE INFLUENTIAL PEEPS

Although there are many types of intended results from God, the last type discussed here are those with the ability to provide guidance to others. These folks provide direction (instruction), help others set goals, and empower others to accomplish great things. (The definition for great things varies among God's children, so don't get hung up when your great things don't look like the *Deliberately Her* great things.)

Who comes to mind when you think of Influential Peeps? This person can influence and motivate others to follow a better path. They can effectively rally the troops for completing various deliverables, whether at church, work, or home. They possess qualities that can be used for influence, persuasion, and empowerment of others. For example, maybe you finally completed your degree or opened the coffee shop you've always wanted because of their advice, influence, and support.

A good example of someone with this ability is Moses. Yes, I am aware he didn't think he was eloquent enough to even speak for God, but Moses still trusted Him. Moses wasn't a great leader because he was a brilliant man with great ideas. Moses was a great leader because he learned to let someone else lead him. He was wise enough to listen to someone with wisdom. He allowed himself to be led by God in order to provide the right leadership to God's people.

If this is you, then one of your qualities is the awareness to be a good follower. And, just so you know, I would love to insert the entire book of Proverbs here, but instead, I will list a few Scriptures to assist you with leading by following:

- **PROVERBS 1:7 (MSG):** *Start with God—the first step in learning is bowing down to God; only fools thumb their noses at such wisdom and learning.*
- **PROVERBS 11:14 (NASB):** *Where there is no guidance the people fall, But in abundance of counselors there is victory.*

- **PROVERBS 12:15 (NASB):** *The way of a fool is right in his own eyes, But a wise man is he who listens to counsel.*
- **PROVERBS 15:31-33 (NASB):** *He whose ear listens to the life-giving reproof will dwell among the wise. He who neglects discipline despises himself, but he who listens to reproof acquires understanding. The fear of the Lord is the instruction for wisdom, and before honor comes humility.*
- **PROVERBS 19:20 (NASB):** *Listen to counsel and accept discipline, That you may be wise the rest of your days.*

Did you notice from the Scriptures that effective leaders lead by learning to seek guidance and support from others? If this is you, I am sure at times of following and leading, you face difficulties with uncertainty because you do not always have the answers. When you do provide guidance, it may not always be 100% accurate. This is okay, because even godly leaders don't have all the answers and are going to make mistakes along the way. Godly leaders understand the word *apologize,* even in circumstances when they're not in the wrong. These folks understand everything cannot always be their way but look to be inclusive and seek what's best for everyone (through the direction of good counsel). Great leaders want unison in addition to order.

If this is you, then you know there is always room for improvement, that will elevate you and enable you to assist others. Remember, the Lord will continue to use you in various ways. It is important to allow yourself to keep learning from whomever God places in your path. I will go as far as to say it is okay for you to *Deliberately Lead!*

Deliberately leading is what you were gifted to do. Your passion in leading is to steer your sheep away from danger and to places of power. Effective power does not intend to control people but to empower them to empower others. If you're leading in a godly way, then it will become an infectious cycle of empowerment. Your ability to lead will create other leaders with the ability to lead. Yes, the last sentence is repetitive but so true! You should desire the best for those around you, and aspire to guide others where they can grow, flourish, and lead someone else one day. You may not always have the solution, but you probably know someone who does. You also understand you will not live forever nor always be a leader in this current moment. This means you understand the importance of continually seeking wisdom and direction from others, so the Kingdom of God can continue to birth great leaders for the next generations of disciples of Christ.

MATTHEW 28:18-20 (MSG):

Jesus, undeterred, went right ahead and gave his charge: "God authorized and commanded me to commission you: **Go out and train everyone you meet, far and near, in this way of life**, *marking them by baptism in the threefold name: Father, Son, and Holy Spirit. Then instruct them in the practice of all I have commanded you. I'll be with you as you do this, day after day after day, right up to the end of the age."* (Emphasis mine)

Conclusion

You should be proud of yourself. You have completed actions intended to help you live more *Deliberately You*. Some of you may have preferred more content for the *how*, but this journey was never intended to be a novel. It was intended to inspire the women of God to seek Him first for assistance with your struggles of just being you.

I hope you have learned what God's view of deliberately means, and that you have discovered an abundance of positive things about yourself. You have a light that God purposely placed in you to support, serve, inspire, and comfort others. You cannot accomplish this if you are deliberately trying to be anyone else but you.

I hope you will use His direction and the Scriptures mentioned throughout the book to think differently about yourself and other people.

I hope you've learned your quirks and thought process were not a mistake, but the intentions of a Father who created you to be comfortable with being you. You will be living with yourself for a long time, and I think it's about time you learned to love who you are.

I hope you know the love of God is bigger than anything you may face, and He purposely intended to shape a *Deliberately You!*

Discussion Questions

CHAPTER 1: *DELIBERATE*

1. Why did you buy this book or what was the reason someone purchased it for you?
2. Are you able to identify with the Introduction? If so, what items stood out for you? What would you identify as present-day issues among women?
3. Do you think Christian women fall easily for worldly norms/structures/behaviors? Why?
4. Do you struggle with being different (deliberate)? If so, how?
5. List things or areas in which you attempt to be deliberate.

CHAPTER 2: *DELIBERATELY HER*

1. Answer these questions honestly. Is there at least one woman you envy? If so, what are the things you envy about her?
2. What were you taught about women from your mother, father, or others in your life?
3. Were they right, or did they have bad experiences that were passed along to you and affected your belief system?
4. How can you embrace the woman who is the *Deliberately Her* in your life? Perhaps she is not as bad as you think, and you can learn from her strengths? List a few.
5. Name four things you like about yourself.

CHAPTER 3: *DELIBERATELY CONFIDENT*

1. Do you walk with your head up or down? What did you learn about the descriptions of how people walk? Did this make you want to change something about yourself?

2. List people you feel are both worldly and godly confident. Identify the differences.

3. On a scale from one to ten, where is your self-esteem? Why?

4. Find, meditate, and go forth with Scriptures pertaining to what the Word says about you.

   a. PHILIPPIANS 4:13 (NIV): *I can do all this through him who gives me strength.*

   b. PSALM 46:5 (NIV): *God is within her, she will not fall; God will help her at break of day.*

   c. ROMANS 5:8 (NIV): *But God demonstrates his own love for us in this: While we were still sinners, Christ died for us.*

   d. 2 TIMOTHY 1:7 (AMP): *For God did not give us a spirit of timidity or cowardice or fear, but [He has given us a spirit] of power and of love and of sound judgment and personal discipline [abilities that result in a calm, well-balanced mind and self-control].*

   e. PSALM 139:13-16 (MSG): *Oh yes, you shaped me first inside, then out; you formed me in my mother's womb. I thank you, High God—you're breathtaking! Body and soul, I am marvelously made! I worship in adoration—what a creation! You know me inside and out, you know every bone in my body; You know exactly how I was made, bit by bit, how I was sculpted from nothing into something. Like an open book, you watched me grow from conception to birth; all the stages of my life were spread out before you, the days of my life all prepared before I'd even lived one day.*

5. How can you allow Christ to make you more *Deliberately Confident* (through Him)?

CHAPTER 4: *DELIBERATELY FAITHFUL*

1. List a few things God has deliberately done in your life? Were you able to identify at the time His faithfulness, and Him as a promise keeper or protector from your self-inflicted destruction?

2. Remember the definition of *faithfulness* as "deserving of trust" on page 50? Have you always trusted God? What usually happens when you don't trust Him? Better yet, how has this affected your decision-making?

3. How has your journey of trusting God evolved? How are your actions different from the above question?

4. Do you think God's faithfulness changes when you do not trust Him? How can you change to show the Lord you will trust Him?

CHAPTER 5: *DELIBERATELY CREATED*

1. How would you describe God as Creator?

2. Now that you have read Chapter 5, how would you describe the word *new*?

3. Identify one action for each item below that you will begin doing for the Kingdom (and yourself).
   a. Prosper
   b. Reproduce
   c. Fill the Earth
   d. Take Charge

CHAPTER 6: *DELIBERATELY ME!*

1. Were you able to identify yourself in the short list of *Deliberately Me* behaviors (Great Listeners, Humble Workers, Friendly Folks, Sympathetic Hearts, Influential Peeps)? If so, which one are you?

2. Have you ever taken a personality or a spiritual gifts test? If not, take them both. You might be able to find free

versions on the Internet. Discuss the results with a close friend or the group.

3. Based on the test results, what are you going to start being more deliberate about?

4. Pray over your action items, and post Scriptures in your house or on the job to influence you in being more deliberate in loving others and yourself.

About the Author

Lee Johnson was born and raised in Canton, Ohio, known to many as home of the Pro Football Hall of Fame. She graduated from McKinley Senior High School and attended Akron University, Columbus State, and Franklin University. She obtained her Associate's degree from Columbus State Community College and completed her Bachelor's degree at Franklin University.

Lee lives with her three daughters—Dejahne, Tahlia, and Izzie (her cat). She enjoys anything cardio from Hip/Hop Zumba, exercising on the elliptical machine, walking, and working out at the Title Boxing Club. Her favorite dessert really is chocolate cake!

Lee desires to share the Word of God through her writing. She hopes to eventually travel the globe to help women ministries develop more women disciples.

Lee eagerly anticipates the continuation of God sharing His vision with her so that she can help you, herself, and many others to continue growing in the knowledge of Jesus Christ. She may be contacted at leejohnson@deliberatelymeseries.com.

Made in the
USA
Lexington, KY

55281573R00055